THE LOOK

THE LOOK

An Around-the-World Fashion

Coloring Book

by
Suwa

Workman Publishing
New York

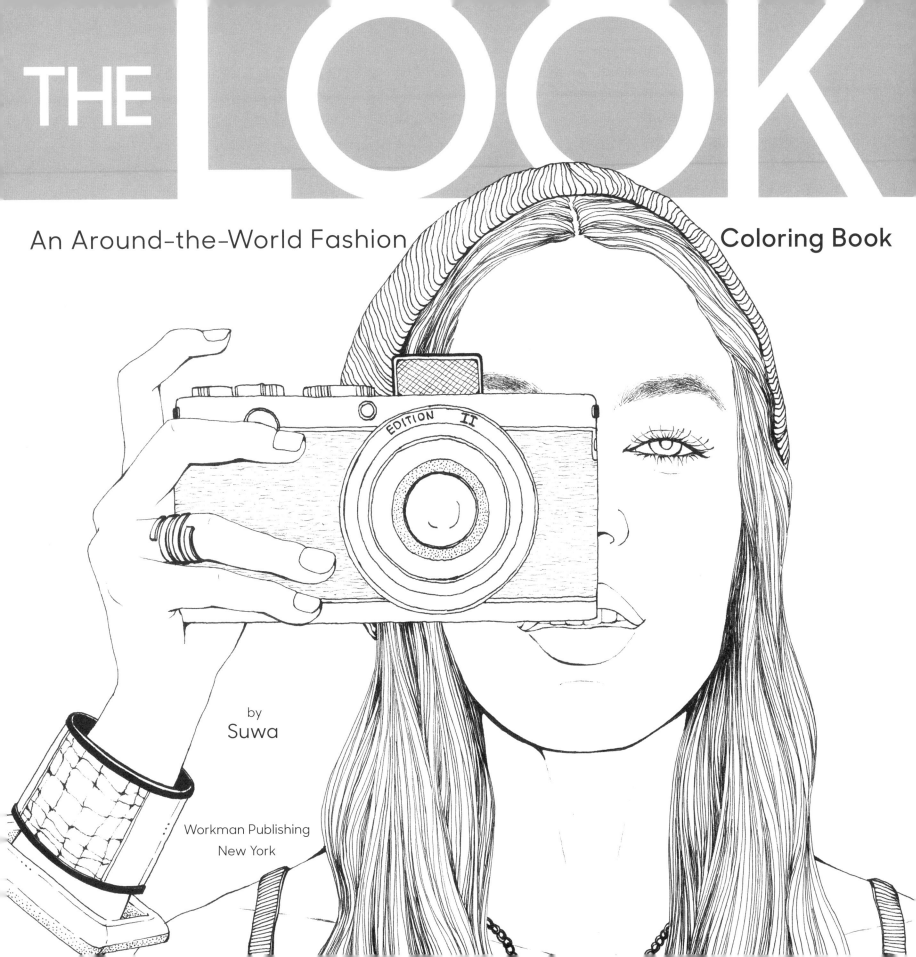

Library of Congress Cataloging-in-Publication Data is available.

ISBN 978-0-7611-8930-5

Workman books are available at special discounts when purchased in bulk for
premiums and sales promotions as well as for fund-raising or educational use.
Special editions or book excerpts can also be created to specification. For details,
contact the Special Sales Director at the address below, or send an email to
specialmarkets@workman.com.

Workman Publishing Co., Inc.
225 Varick Street
New York, New York 10014-4381
workman.com

WORKMAN is a registered trademark of Workman Publishing Co., Inc.

Printed in Mexico
First printing September 2015

LOOK

this book
belongs to

Jada

Shanghai

Tokyo

Seoul

PARIS

ANTWERP

LONDON

MILAN

PIZZERIA
CON SERVIZIO DI CUCINA

STOCKHOLM

NEW YORK

SHANGHAI

TOKYO

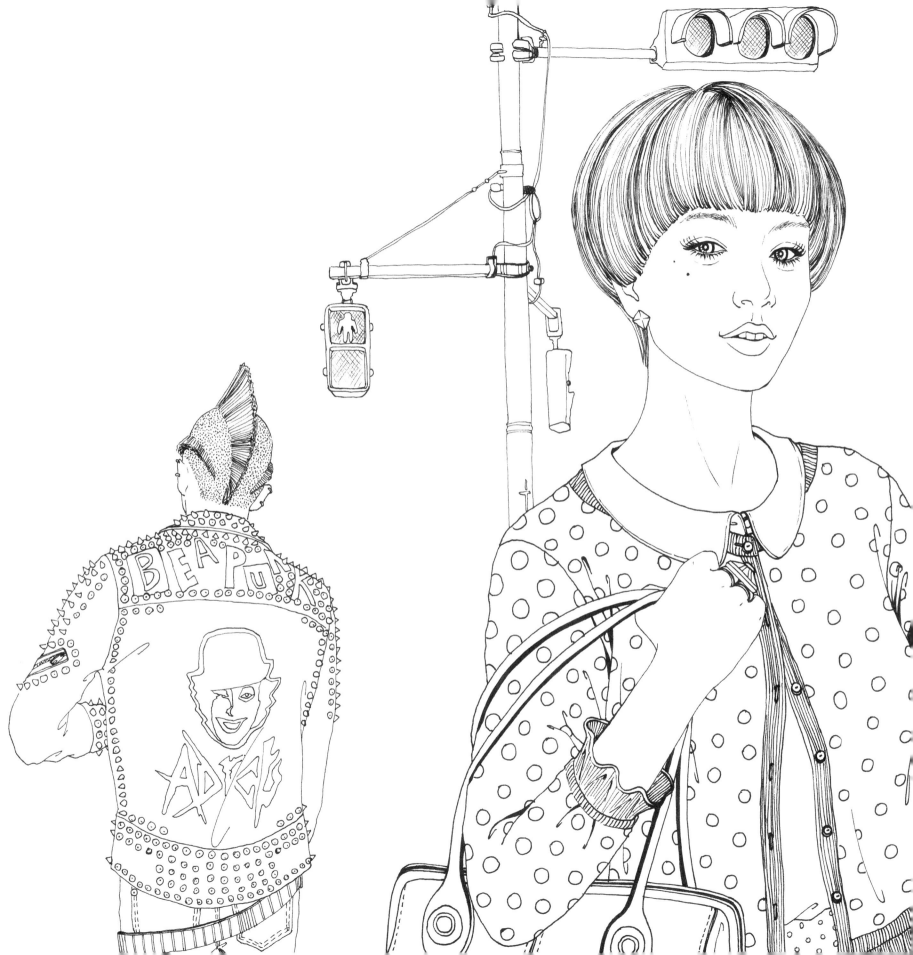

SEOUL

ENJOY THE STREET LOOK

ABOUT THE ARTIST

Suwa studied fashion at Parsons School of Design and worked as a fashion designer for Michael Kors and Tommy Hilfiger. She now lives in South Korea, where she's worked as an art director and lecturer.